I Have

Talents,

and I Am Not

Afraid to

Use Them

R. Shawnté Jones

Acknowledgments

"In everything give thanks; for this is the will of God in Christ Jesus for you."

—1 Thessalonians 5:18

I would like to give thanks to God for what He has given me and for what He does for me each day. I thank those who have supported me in my endeavors and have believed in me regardless of the situation. Your support means so much to me. To my parents, I thank you for being who you are and for allowing me to be who I am.

Contents

Introduction

Don't let the past ruin your life by
letting it run your life!

You are more than what you think!

Introduction

Nothing splendid has ever been achieved except by those who dared believe that something inside them was superior to circumstances.

—*Bruce Barton*

Completing this book has been a goal of mine for the past few years. Throughout the time I was working on it, I kept hitting mental blocks. One of these was the concern about whether anyone would be interested in reading what I write. So, I would wait until the end of the year and try to push myself to finish before the close of the year, just to miss the impractical deadline, and then put off working on writing for months. I finally got to the realization that, although what I am writing could potentially help someone, I need to finish this book for myself. I told myself that I need to work on writing with the same intensity and drive that I used when working on writing assignments for school. I would devote hours to working on school assignments, and I asked myself: Why am I not as dedicated to completing this book? It boiled down to acceptance, appreciation, and fear of failure.

I began working on the ideas for this book in 2011. What ignited my desire to write this book in particular was the scripture about the talents found in Matthew 25:14–18 (NKJV):

> *14 For the kingdom of heaven is like a man traveling to a far country, who called his own servants and delivered his goods to them. 15 And to one he gave five talents, to another two, and to another one, to each according to his own ability; and immediately he went on a journey. 16 Then he who had received the five talents went and traded with them, and made another five talents. 17 And likewise he who had received two gained two more also. 18 But he who had received one went and dug in the ground, and hid his lord's money.*

I had read this scripture multiple times when reading my Bible; however, a few years ago, at a funeral, these were the key verses, and they stood out to me. This was in 2011 when I thought to begin work on this book. I have forgotten what was preached about at the funeral; however, when I read those verses again, the way I felt during the funeral came back to me. WARNING: This book is not meant to be a literal interpretation of the parable of the talents found in the aforementioned verses. This book is a representation of how

Introduction

I interpreted the verses and what I took away from the parable, which was the lack of using talent. Because the servant was afraid, he hid it. His fear caused him to not make progress, and the result was that he became further behind because what he had was taken away and given to someone else. Many of us are like that servant, hiding our talents because we are afraid of something.

I believe that God has equipped us all with some type of talent, and some of us received several that are intended to further advance His kingdom. We all have a purpose, and it's up to each of us to discover how to use what has been given. Fear and criticism should not keep us from using our God-given talents. God gave you the talent, so don't let others talk you out of using it.

As I reflect on the use of my talents, those that I have worked on over the years as well as those that have yet to be developed, I think back to when I was younger. I loved to draw and write. I could come up with a story idea from almost any situation. I would get lost in writing. The same was the case with drawing. I would draw houses, vehicles, and landscapes, but mostly I drew people. I probably had well over fifty drawings of fictional people that I created off the top of my head. I recall being very pleased with those drawings. With each person that I drew, I created a story in my head about him or her. The pivotal moment came in my life when, on one summer day, some relatives criticized my drawings and picked them apart. They had fun laughing at my artwork. I was crushed. I was in junior high at the time, and hearing such criticism about something that I was so passionate about was more than what I knew how to properly handle. I didn't say anything to them about it, because I was hurt, and I started to criticize the artwork myself. Not long after, I threw away all of my drawings, and the only time I drew after that was in art class.

That moment of hearing my work being needlessly criticized impacted my other creative activities, such as writing. I continued to write, but I became very protective of my writings. I didn't want anyone to read what I wrote because of my fear of criticism. It took years for me to overcome that fear, and I still hesitate to openly share my work. Writing and publishing this book is more than a goal accomplished for me. It is conquering a fear.

As time went on, it became clear to me that everyone will not appreciate my talents—at an amateur or professional level. Hiding my talents or abandoning them completely was harmful to me and my overall development. Licking the wounds of my shattered confidence was not helping me or anyone else. I was bruised, but my abilities were not destroyed.

Introduction

So I am writing this book not because I am an expert (I am an expert in my own situations) but because I want to encourage others to take their talents off the shelf, dig them up, or, better yet, to never stop developing the ability to use their talents. The following pages are a combination of what I have learned along my journey, either via my own experiences or in observation of the experiences of others. All of this I wish I had known back when I was in junior high.

I know there are others who have experienced a similar situation to mine, with criticism and the reaction to it. My reaction was by far not the correct response, and I hope that sharing what I learned will provide ideas to others on how to handle their own situations.

I hope that readers of this book experience a spark to ignite their dreams, to use their talents, and to encourage others to do so as well. They are your talents. You are not using them for someone else. Make the most out of what is yours. Treat them as prized possessions. God wants you to use your talents. Honor Him. Remember that you were given that talent for a reason. It is for you to determine how you will go about using it.

Success

Happy are those who live their own lives!

Success

If your success is not on your terms, if it looks good to the world but does not feel good in your heart, it is not success at all.

—Anna Quindlen

If at first you don't succeed, should you try again? The old saying, "If at first you don't succeed, try again," may not always apply to every situation. You should ask yourself if you should try again.

Every mountain that you see isn't meant for you to climb. Every challenge that you face is not for you to overcome. You may find that you are going through difficulties and adversity because you are trying to do something that is not intended for you to do. Are you going after your dreams and goals or someone else's?

Assess the Situation

Are you pursuing a goal that you feel passionate about? Sometimes as you are trying to figure out which way to go in your life, which career to choose, you may find yourself going after a career that someone else wants you to pursue. This sometimes happens with high-school graduates who are unsure of career opportunities or of what they want to do in life. Their parents then step in and direct their educational future, including the college that the graduate attends.

At times, this is based on the experiences of the parents and not always what the parent sees as potential in the child. Parents sometimes want their children to go to the same college as they did or pursue the same career as they are in. Or maybe they hate their career choices and work to steer their children in the opposite direction. However, following someone else's path doesn't always set you up for reaching your success.

There is nothing wrong with taking direction or guidance from others; it is actually encouraged. However, in doing so, you should make sure that what you are pursuing is in alignment with what you have a genuine interest in pursuing and developing. What is it that you keep going back to, either mentally or physically?

You can eliminate years of frustration by making choices based on what you believe is right for you; what you have a passion for; and what you have the knowledge, skills, and abilities to do.

Listen to Feedback and Own It

When I was interviewing for a new position several years ago, the hiring manager gave me what I consider is good advice. Immediately after my interview, she and I had lunch, and she asked me about my career goals. I informed her that I eventually would like to get into learning and development. To my surprise, she observed during the interview that when I spoke about anything related to training or facilitating, my face lit up, and I became really animated. She said that it's hard to find someone in our field who truly wants to facilitate and has a gift for facilitation. Several days later, she informed me that she was going to pursue other candidates for the job she was trying to fill. To paraphrase her feedback to me, she advised that I should focus my efforts on what I truly have a gift and passion for and not pursue a change just because it seems like the natural next step in my career. I have held on to that advice, and it's the same advice that I will give to anyone who is willing to listen.

Not long after this conversation, I had the opportunity to present information at a poster session on employee development. On the second day, I met a consultant on public speaking, and he and I chatted about the differences in presenting and facilitating. I was intrigued by the conversation and let him know that I would like to know whether I present or facilitate. He committed to stopping by when I spoke and would let me know. As promised, he stopped by when I was speaking, and afterward I went to him to find out how I did. He commended me on my facilitation skills and on my ability to draw the audience in to participating. He told me that facilitation is a gift of leadership and that I was really good at it. My confidence took a big leap!

There was also a senior vice-president who listened in on one of my poster sessions, and he thought it was great and wanted more information. At the end of the day, after all of the events had wrapped up, one of the participants came to me and stated that I was the best presenter of all the posters that she visited and that participants were recommending to other participants to stop by the poster. When I reflected on the events of both days, I remember feeling a sense of accomplishment and pure excitement from being at the poster sessions and the recognition from others that validated that this is a gift and a talent that I naturally have and enjoy using. Of course, as with anything, I have to continue to develop and get better.

Interestingly, when I had to give presentations when I first started college, I felt really uncomfortable and hated it. Fortunately, I kept being thrust into opportunities to present. Partly because my continuous education required it and also because, on the job, my coworkers were not enthusiastic about presenting, the opportunities landed in my lap. By the time I finished my graduate degree, I was much better at presenting and facilitating and was enthusiastic about doing so.

When you truly have a gift, people will recognize it without you having to try hard. You will naturally get in the zone. Sometimes that can be dangerous. I got caught in my confidence in being a good facilitator. In working to get the approval to facilitate a personal effectiveness workshop, I didn't take the time to thoroughly practice the material before the test run. I kept putting it off, and then I went on vacation the week leading up to the test run.

"Preparation and effort are requirements for all endeavors."

When it was time for the test run, my lack of preparation showed in that I wasn't well versed in the content. Though I did a good job in working the room and had the appropriate level of energy, our trainers stopped me within the first five minutes and drilled me. I was deflated, and it seemed as if the critique wouldn't end. Later at dinner, I was complimented on my abilities and received additional constructive feedback, but it was reinforced that I couldn't skim over the content, because that was the important piece of the facilitation.

I mention these experiences for two reasons. The first is that it doesn't matter how good you are or how good you think you are; preparation is necessary if you want others to take you seriously. Success doesn't come if you are not genuine. Success doesn't come when others depend on you and you are not giving them your best. Being held accountable and suffering from embarrassment were lessons that I likely won't forget. Don't take advantage of being good at doing something and think that it will always work out without having to properly prepare. Preparation and effort are requirements for all endeavors.

The second reason I mention these experiences is because at one time, I didn't believe myself to be any good in presenting or facilitating. Any negative feedback that I have received and occasionally still receive from some people brings about doubt and uncertainty about what I have to offer. In addition to preparation, prior to going into an endeavor that you want to achieve success, you must believe in yourself and to be able to discern what feedback to throw away and what feedback you should keep. As tough or as harsh as it may seem, everyone is not interested in seeing you to being successful.

Visualize Yourself Being Successful

Define what success looks like for you. Only you can define what success looks like for you. Only you can determine if you reach it. Each person is motivated by different rewards, so success defined by one person doesn't have to mean success for you. I participated in an activity where we were told to draw what success looked like. Almost everyone had a completely different picture. No one had a wrong answer, because if you are defining your success, then it's all about you. So don't let others tell you that you are or are not successful based on their measuring stick. You must use your own measuring stick. Run your own race. Only detour if doing so is of benefit to you.

How happy would you be if you were pursuing a degree or certification in a field that you had no talent or passion to pursue? The answer is that you would likely not put forth the effort to do well in your studies or in your career, which you will find dreadful. Don't try to force yourself into doing something that you are not equipped to do. It will lead to frustration and will deplete your happiness and confidence levels.

If you are going into a new situation and can't visualize yourself being successful at it, then you may want to ask yourself why you are pursuing it. You are in a no-win situation, and the road ahead is bound to be unremarkable and mediocre at best. However, when you are working in your talent, you will do great things. This is where you will achieve success.

Of course, we will all have to do things that we don't like. But the great news is that there are people who probably enjoy doing those things, so if you can delegate, delegate so that you can get to doing the things that you enjoy and find your success.

Before You Go...

As you run this race of life, consider it a marathon versus a sprint, and remember that in the competition of success, you are only competing against yourself. Therefore, before starting any endeavor, you should define what success looks like for you. Once you reach that, celebrate, and then move on to the next thing.

Mentoring Relationships

Turn a no into a yes by moving forward and doing your best!

Mentoring Relationships

Trust someone who has tried.

—Virgil

Having a mentor can provide many benefits to you. However, the relationship should be mutually beneficial to you and your mentor. The benefits will likely not be the same, but both the mentor and mentee should feel that the experience is rewarding. That is why having the right mentor is important.

My Mentor Relationship Experience

When I was first introduced to the concept of mentoring, I was actually turned down by someone who was recommended to me. I worked in an office environment as an administrative specialist. Though I didn't know exactly what

I wanted to do in my career at that time, I knew that my long-term goals did not include remaining in an administrative specialist role. I was actually pursuing my bachelor of arts degree in communication in hopes of becoming a communication specialist once I completed the degree. However, I still had several years to go before I completed my degree, so I wasn't quite ready for a move yet.

One of my coworkers who knew of my desires to break out of the administrative specialist role suggested that I get a mentor. She gave me the name of someone whom she thought would be a good fit for me. This individual was once an administrative specialist and had received a number of promotions and was now in a technical role. As I did not know this individual, although we worked for the same company, my coworker who had suggested her offered to reach out to my potential mentor for me.

I was in disbelief at how this situation unfolded. Turns out this individual had no desire to mentor me. Although this was many years ago, I still remember the voice mail message that she left for me. Yes, a voice mail. She stated, "Since you are an admin, you need to get a mentor who is an admin. I am not an admin." I was furious. Though I didn't know much about mentoring at the time, I knew enough to know that you don't have to work in the same occupation as someone in order to have a mentoring relationship. I also knew, judging by the attitude that was presented in the voice mail, that I didn't want someone to mentor me who seemed to look down on my occupation.

I did end up connecting with someone else but found that she was dismissive as well. We had one meeting, and she gave me a list of things to do and basically told me that there was no need for us to meet again. To give them both the benefit of the doubt, maybe they didn't know much about mentoring either and didn't want to put themselves on the spot by taking on such a role. I will never know.

After these two incidents occurred, I became leery and skeptical of the idea of having a mentor, but I tried again with someone who was signed up in the mentoring program. That didn't work, either. I ended that relationship because I was discouraged by the others and didn't have much faith in the program. Now that I am more experienced and have worked my way out of an administrative specialist role, I know the value of having a mentor and would encourage everyone to get one—no matter where you are in life or in your career.

Fortunately for me, several years after I switched companies, I was able to get a mentor who was very valuable to me. This relationship began as a result of a formal mentorship program at the company. I signed up to get a mentor through an internal online program. I was matched with two people after I answered all of the questions. I picked my mentor when the two selections were produced, and she reached out to me to confirm acceptance of the role.

This relationship was much more than what I expected. As mentioned previously, my attempts at having a mentor were failures. My mentor asked me questions and provided me with recommendations. Throughout the relationship we had well-rounded conversations. She was the reason that I was able to start participating in some organizational development activities.

Selfishly, I was disappointed when I found out she was retiring. I finally had someone to show me the ropes, and now she was leaving me; that was what I thought. She pointed me in the right direction that gave me a boost that I needed. After almost five years with the company, I was able to visit other sites and interact with coworkers on some of the more visible organizational development interventions going on at the time. I got this exposure because of my mentor.

Everyone is not cut out to be your mentor, and you should know what to look out for. There are many traits that a mentor should possess. Some are listed below.

Your mentor:

- Should have your best interest in mind when giving you advice.

- Must be someone you respect. It is difficult to have a healthy and effective interpersonal relationship with someone whom you do not respect. It doesn't make sense to try to have a relationship with someone who doesn't exhibit the same morals, ethics, or values as you do.

- Must be someone you are willing to follow. This is not saying that you need to be anyone's shadow or puppet. It also doesn't mean that the path that person took to get to where he or she is now is the right path for you. This means that the person is someone whom you deem to make the right decisions, or rather, the best decision he or she can under the given circumstances.

- Should be someone who has already been "there." This person can relate or give guidance based on his or her experience. Ideally, the person you have as your mentor should have relatable experiences that you can learn from.

- Should help you develop your talents.

- Should believe in you. This relationship should not be a check-mark exercise.

- Should introduce you to new opportunities or new ways to do things.

- Should motivate you mentally, emotionally, and spiritually, depending on the relationship.

- Should want to help you.

- Should be someone who can connect with you. Even if the experience seems right, the chemistry that you have with your mentor may not be. This doesn't mean that one person is bad. A mentoring relationship is just like any other relationship. You have to be able to connect with each other. The connection will help you to feel comfortable when opening up. The connections serves as a catalyst to good communication.

- Should not lead you astray. Your mentor should be smart enough to help you to avoid costly mishaps. This is in recognition that as a human being who is capable of reasoning and making your own decisions, you will, at times, make mistakes. However, these mistakes should not be based on misguided direction from your mentor.

It may be that a mentor may come to you unsolicited. Sometimes these relationships dissolve as quickly as they start. A person may take you under his or her wing for a project or witness you going through something he or she has experienced before. This experience puts this person in a position to be able to help you, and he

"You have to be able to connect with each other."

or she takes the opportunity to do so. Occasionally, mentor relationships are informal, and the mentee doesn't realize that the person who stops by every now and then and offers advice or the person who encourages the mentee to speak up is acting as a mentor. It's not necessary to have a formal title.

If you find that your mentor is not working for you, then you should respectfully end the relationship. Regardless of who your mentor is, you should not remain in a relationship that is not good for you.

Before You Go...

There is no one right way to have a mentoring relationship. You can have one mentor or five mentors, whatever works for you. However, you should remember that the key ingredient is that this is a relationship, and you should treat it as such.

Recognizing Your Talents

Make the most out of today by using what you learned yesterday.

Recognizing Your Talents

Never let what you cannot do, interfere with what you can do.

—*John Wooden*

In recognizing your talents, it may take a series of trial and error to find out exactly what you are good at. As in the parable that this book references, you may find that you are talented at a number of things, and that's fine. However, you need to understand how each talent works with the others. You may find that you can't use one when you use the other. You may also find that just because you can do something doesn't mean that you are talented at it.

Leave it to the Experts

Several years ago, I hosted a career management event. I was excited about the event and nervous all in one. I was excited because the concepts of career management are of great interest to me, and I believe that in understanding how to manage your career, you are setting yourself up for success. I recognized that during the previous years of my awareness on the subject that no offerings of such a seminar had taken place in the community, and I wanted to expose individuals to the concepts. Mind you, I am aware that various companies offer development classes on the topic, but I wanted to have a seminar that touched on a variety of career management topics that was available to anyone who didn't have that opportunity with his or her employer.

The slate of speakers was great, the topics and activities were on point for what I wanted, the venue was great, there were snacks and drinks, but where were the people? In hindsight, I realized that to organize such an event, it's not a one-person job. One of my speakers stated to me that she learned that there are some things that you need to let professionals do. That statement and other moments of reflection allowed me to recognize that I need the help of others to help me in areas that I am not gifted in.

Can I organize an event? Yes. Can I get speakers for events? Yes. Can I use social media to get the word out? Yes, but not effectively. It's easy to post to your pages and send invites to the masses, but yet another matter to get people interested and flowing in. Can I design promotional items and brochures? Yes, but they lack the eye-catching power that someone with graphic design experience can create. Can I sell tickets? Yes, to my family and friends.

What I am saying here is that I recognize that I have the capabilities to do a lot of things to host an event; however, I am not gifted at all the things that I was trying to do to make it a successful event in regards to advertising and ticket sales. My lack of these gifts showed in attendance— great events, but low attendance. I realized that I need to leave those activities to individuals who have those talents. I recognized that I didn't have those talents by trial and error. For me, it took two costly events to teach me that lesson. So now, in the planning stages of an event, I have soliciting volunteers as one of my to-do items because I have learned that marketing is not a developed skill set for me.

To recognize your talents, you can start off by looking at your hobbies or the things that you enjoy doing. What are the activities that you gladly volunteer for or that you find yourself doing in your spare time? For some, it's easy to pick these activities out, but for others, depending on your overall life responsibilities, you may find that you do what's necessary and not necessarily what is fun.

There are a number of assessment tools available to get you thinking about your career path and tell you what your hobbies ought to be based on your personality. However, those assessments are not always accurate, but you can use them as a reference. Assessments are good if you are unsure of what works for you in order to begin to explore what you are good at. They can be used as a good starting point.

Assessing Your Abilities

As you continue your journey of recognizing your talents, it is important that, while doing so, you assess your abilities. This goes beyond looking at what you like to do; it lies in honestly assessing your strengths and weaknesses. We all have strengths, and we all have weaknesses. We can call the weaknesses opportunities for development or deadweight. It depends on the role they play in your life and in your future.

Another measuring stick to discovering your talents is to think about the activity or activities that you go to over and over again when other activities don't work out. What do you fall back to?

In a previous role, my team was working on a project on our action plans for what we would do in an emergency and making sure we had the right items on hand in case an emergency came about. Our manager divvied everything out. It got to the point where most everyone was making good progress on their action items—all but one person. Our manager decided to take what this person was responsible for and give it to me. After it was completed, my manager stated that he knew that I could get it done. The reward was not only monetary but also his recognition of my organizational abilities. When people recognize that you have the ability to accomplish certain activities effectively, they are more comfortable going to you with their requests, and it pays off for you in the long run.

You have to be careful, though, when people recognize what you are good at. Sometimes when people see certain traits in you, they want to steer you toward what they believe is a logical career choice. Some coworkers have recognized my analytical abilities, attention to detail, and organizational capabilities and recommended that I look into environmental health and safety and into compensation as career options. Neither of those career fields was in my line of sight, and knowing that I was not interested in those career fields, I chose not to pursue either. Those career choices seemed right to others for what I should pursue in my career, but that is not what I believed to be right for me. I do reserve the right to reconsider those options in the future.

"Remember that what God has given to you, He has given it to you."

Find Out About the Experiences of Others

Remember that what God has given to you, He has given it to you. Likewise, what He gave to someone else, He gave to them. If you do not have a desire in your heart to pursue something, then don't. At some point, you may come around to it if it is something for you to pursue, but there is a time for everything. Though others may see something in you that you don't see in yourself, if your heart isn't in it, will you put forth the necessary effort to succeed? Your talents are uniquely yours. Do not take offense to this, but you cannot do effectively what someone else is supposed to do. You may get it done, but was it as good as it could be? And what was the cost to you in doing it (and I am not speaking financially)? It is also important to note that you need to know what God has given to you. Take the time necessary to figure it out. Be willing to talk to people to find out how they recognized their talents. Depending on your environment, you may have to expand your network.

If you are not able to immediately expand your network, you can learn more about other successful individuals. I like to read biographies or to watch television programs that go behind the scenes on how successful people have achieved their success. The challenges they faced. The connections they made and how they made them. Hearing about the number of times they were turned down and then hearing about their big breaks are inspirational. My story is different from their story, but when I listen to their stories, I make notes to myself on how to approach certain situations. If you take the time to listen, you can learn something from everyone.

Finding out more about the history of those whom you consider overcomers can serve as reminders that perseverance, the right connections, confidence, and the unshakable belief in yourself and your abilities will help get you to the next level on your path to discovering your talents, using your talents, and experiencing success in doing so.

Before You Go...

You should always be honest with yourself and determine what you are really good at. It takes time and energy to pretend or operate in a manner that is not suited for you, and it keeps you from doing what you should be doing. Therefore, if you find that you are having trouble recognizing your talent, ask someone you trust for guidance.

Investing in Your Talents

Make a commitment to continuously develop yourself.

Investing in Your Talents

A goal without a plan is just a wish.

—Antoine de Saint-Exupéry

Once you have recognized your talents, it is important to not expect them to work for you without you putting forth any effort. A talent unused is a talent removed. How often have you heard someone refer to being able to once do something, but after a while of not doing it, he or she no longer can? You hear phrases such as: "I used to," "When I was younger, I was able to," and so on.

You never know whether that activity that you used to do well, but can't do anymore, was the talent unused that is now the talent removed. Why not take the time to explore your talents? The time that you spend on anything is an investment, just as spending money on anything is an investment.

By doing research, you will find that the skills you possess can be used in a multitude of ways. You should invest the time to find out how you can use your talents. Avoid being narrow-minded and only focusing on the obvious; think of alternatives and discover different ways for YOU to use your talents.

Carve Out Time to Shape Up Your Talent

If something is truly important to you, does someone have to tell you to make the time to do it? Probably not. If living a healthy lifestyle is important to you, will someone have to drag you off the couch to exercise? The chances are, you are probably trying to encourage someone else to come along with you.

If you've ever seen a world-champion body builder, imagine how that person was able to form such muscles. He or she made time to work out. It took time, effort and energy to get to where he or she is now. There was no magical can of spinach to cause muscles to immediately bulge out. If you were to find a before and after picture of a body builder, you will notice a vast difference. Consider your talents as muscles on a body builder. Just like a body builder, you have to exercise your talents consistently so that they become strong and defined. Eventually you will gain the confidence to flex your talents so that everyone can see what you are made of. Remember that your talents are already in you; you just have to work them out to get them ready to use.

Practice

As the saying goes, "practice makes perfect." It's impossible to get better at something if you don't put any effort into it.

There is a popular dance competition on television where many hopefuls try to make it past the audition phase of the competition. Often many of the dancers have danced their whole lives, and others may only have a handful of years of experience. However, regardless of the length of time they have danced, the judges can determine who has put forth the effort to continue to grow and challenge themselves in their art. It takes more than passion; a number of the dancers eliminated have the passion but not the talent.

Weight loss is the same. In a popular weight-loss competition that has spread into the lives of fans, the contestants often have testimonies of having picked up so much weight by eating unhealthy foods and not making the time to work out. Well, on the show, they have no choice but to work out, because the scale will tell the story. By the finale, it's hard to recognize some of the contestants from their before images. What happened? They invested the time to lose the weight and change their lives. Doing so meant making sacrifices and making their weight loss a priority. Why am I using this example? It goes to show that no matter the hurdle that you face, if it's something that you make the time to do and have the will to do, you can conquer it.

Both examples show that no matter what your intention, if you do not follow intention with practice and work at it, no matter how good you are, you ultimately won't succeed. There is no quick win for real success. You must be able to sustain success by continually investing in your talents.

The Olympic Games are a perfect opportunity to witness how practicing pays off. There is much hype surrounding the events; whether a given activity is taking place on stage, field, or pool, we are amazed at the talents displayed. Why? Because we have the opportunity to witness the best of the best in athletics. How do these athletes reach elite status, you may ask? Practice. Some of these athletes spend their entire lives practicing in order to continue to sharpen their skills and abilities. In order to work with the best trainers, some of these Olympians will leave their families and fully focus on their specialties. It's probably safe to say that these athletes practice, compete, practice, win, and repeat until they choose to retire.

This is not to say that you need to operate on the same level as an Olympian. This is saying that, depending on what you want to accomplish, you will have to put forth the equivalent work in order to get there. Success doesn't just happen overnight. You will need to be willing to invest the precious commodity of time to prepare yourself.

Increase Your Knowledge With Continuous Education

Get an advanced degree: If the area of your talent offers an advanced degree, go for it. This will allow you to explore other additional components of the field. You are already equipped with the foundational knowledge, but with an advanced degree, you are taking a deeper dive into the subject matter. You will have the opportunity to learn more about it, which will likely uncover information that you were not aware of. Believe me, I know.

Before pursuing my master of science degree in human resource development, I was fully intent on gaining enough knowledge to prepare myself to become a learning and development specialist. However, since going through the program and learning more about organizational development, I have shifted my interest. This is something that others in the program expressed as well. The more you know, the more you grow, and the more aware you become of what's available to you.

Attend seminars: Making time and spending the money to go to seminars are valuable in a number of ways. While you are learning more about the subject matter, you are also surrounded by other individuals who are also interested in the subject matter. This is a great networking opportunity. Seminars also allow for you to keep up with trends and new techniques, all of which you can use as you continue to shape your talents to best work for you.

Obtain certifications: Often, once formal schooling is complete, many who have entered into their career fields of choice have no desire to go back to school. They become satisfied with where they are and what they have accomplished. They become comfortable. However, becoming certified in a specialized area increases your knowledge about your subject matter and keeps you informed of relevant changes and advancements.

"It's about what you do with what you learn."

Getting certified shows commitment and is an investment. As with almost anything, the area of your talent is ever-changing and in order for you to remain successful, you must change with it. Otherwise, what you have to offer becomes irrelevant and opportunities that were once coming your way will go to someone else.

Certifications, attending seminars and earning degrees are costly, but they are worth it when you are investing in your talent zone. Before you make the financial investment, make sure you are investing it where you are equipped to be successful. Instruction offers the least payback than any other learning opportunity; however, it is a critical factor in learning more about and developing your talent. It's about what you do with what you learn. Therefore, you must make the most out of every advancement in your knowledge by following it up with action. In order to increase the impact of instructional learning, compound it with action. For example, if you are taking a leadership course, in order to help make your learning stick, seek out opportunities to lead a team, ministry, or organization.

Challenge Yourself

Once you feel that you have reached a level of mastery, challenge yourself by passing on what you know to someone else. You can teach a class, become a mentor, write a book, or create online posts about what you know and your experiences. Doing any of these activities will challenge your thinking and will likely drive you to find out even more about the subject matter. Remember, there is always more to learn!

By investing in your talents, you are continuously sharpening your knowledge, skills, and abilities. You are becoming more valuable to others and to yourself. You also may discover other ways in which you can use your talents. The more you know, the more you grow!

Investing your time and money can move you forward, so don't waste either. Make sure that what you invest in is well planned and that you know in advance what you plan to do with your newfound knowledge. There are plenty of people who have invested the time and money to getting an advanced degree but are doing nothing related to it. Knowing what you want to do with your talents will save you both time and money and will serve as a guide for what and where to invest. Don't plan as you go; plan before you go.

Remember that anything worth having is worth the effort that it will take to get it.

Before You Go...

When you make an investment, it should be for the long-term benefits. Otherwise, it's not really an investment. Understand what it is going to take in order for you improve and live up to your full potential, and then make the commitment to stick with it.

Defending Against Negative Energies

Listen. Think. React.

Defending Against Negative Energies

You can learn anything you need to learn to achieve any goal you set for yourself. There are no limits except the limits you place on your imagination.

—Brian Tracy

As you move forward with working within your talents, you must prepare yourself for the potential negative energies that will come your way. Negative energies can come from many different directions, including from you. Yes, I said it. You, yourself, can bring about negative energies via thoughts, words, and actions that will inhibit you from using the talents you have.

Your Negative Thoughts are Weighing You Down

Negative thoughts may enter your mind without notice. It's important for you to recognize these thoughts and program your mind to dismiss them. It's easy to think about what didn't work before, but focusing on past failures is not a productive activity. If those thoughts keep creeping up, start thinking about how you can turn those past failures into future successes. Find the learning opportunities in every situation.

To help boost yourself up from drowning in negative thoughts, be ready to remind yourself of past successes and accomplishments. You should take actions to help build your confidence. Below are some suggestions that you should try.

Have a "way to go" folder or file: This is a collection of goals that you have achieved, accomplishments, letters of recognition, congratulatory letters, or any other documentation that you have that applauds your success. You can even include copies of diplomas, degrees, or certifications that you have received. This will allow you to go back and see proof of your past successes. So if you find yourself down in the dumps, you can use this file as a reference to get back on track. Despite your background or upbringing, you have experienced some level of success. Start tracking your successes, great and small. Once you start keeping a list of your successes, you will be amazed at how much you have accomplished.

Have a support network: There is nothing like having a group of people who support your efforts and believe in your ability to achieve success. You want to make sure your support network is made up of people who are sincere in their support. These are people you can go to as needed to remind you to stay positive and encourage you to move forward.

Practice, practice, practice: You want to make sure you practice your talent until you are comfortable with it. Just as a baby is unsure of him- or herself when first standing up and trying to walk, you are unsure when you first start using your talents. And just like a baby, the more you try, the better you get. Babies don't give up, and you shouldn't, either.

Refer to what's worked before: This goes back to having a "way to go" folder. However, if you choose to not have a folder, you can mentally reflect back on what has worked. You should have a long-term memory of your past accomplishments. This can help you to mentally remind yourself of what you can do and give you a burst of energy to keep charging forward on getting better at your talent. Of course, what worked in the past may not work in your current situation, so use this as a reference.

Celebrate your accomplishments: Don't let your accomplishments go unnoticed. When you overcome a challenge or achieve a goal, you should take a moment to celebrate those accomplishments. This doesn't mean you should take a long break in celebration, but this is you taking the time to recognize and reward yourself for what you have accomplished. You can have small celebrations for milestones and big celebrations for overall goal achievement. Knowing that a celebration is coming can serve as a source of motivation.

Pay it forward: A good source of motivation is taking the time to share with others what you have learned. When you have the opportunity to work with others or show others how to do something that you have achieved or are good at, this provides an internal reward for yourself. You make others feel good when you spend time with them, and it offers a feel-good moment for you as well.

Turn to God for inspiration: Remember to thank God for your talents and praise Him for having His hand in your life. As it says in Luke 1:37, "For with God nothing will be impossible."

Your Negative Words are Holding You Back

You should be mindful of what you say, as your words can direct your steps. If negative words are coming out of your mouth, someone may hear you and make judgments about you based on them. Everything that comes to mind doesn't need to come out of your mouth. As is says in Proverbs 18:21, "life and death lies in the power of your tongue," so don't speak destruction into your life. Speak positive affirmations into your life.

People are Watching and Listening

Believe it or not, people watch you even when you don't know it. You are always on an interview. People whom you interact with—directly or indirectly—are making an assessment about you. They may see you doing something and make a mental note about it. They may see how you react to bad news and make a mental note. They observe how you take a compliment and how you handle criticism. You never know whose eyes are watching you and whose ears are listening. These people are witnesses to some part of your life and will draw to memory their interactions with you when they see you again or when they hear mention of your name.

When I was attending college, this happened to me. One of my instructors approached me about an opportunity to work at a major corporation as a co-op. This was unsolicited by me because I had a job and was content. However, she saw something in me that led her to believe that I would represent the co-op program well in that organization. She later told me that she saw something in me that she didn't see in the other girls. That opportunity opened the doors for me for many other opportunities. Several years later this same instructor approached me about becoming a part-time instructor at the college and was willing to take me directly to her manager to speak up on my behalf. Again, this was unsolicited.

People who are watching you can use their observations to help elevate you in your interests or career. Their observations can also lead to negative perceptions and a negative reputation. The lesson here is that you should always behave as if you are on an interview. Your behavior speaks volumes about your character. People are more willing to associate their name with yours or take a risk on you if you have shown them that you are worthy of it. If people associate you with trouble, you will have trouble moving forward with your hopes, goals, and dreams.

Remember that everyone is not going to believe in you. Some of these individuals may go as far as being condescending toward you. You are never good enough in their eyes. They may see you as competition, or you may be finding success in an area in which they were not able to succeed. No matter the reason, you must remain focused on what you know is a natural talent or ability and not allow the unbelief of others to deter you from moving forward.

Adversity is a part of life that everyone faces in some measure. The way you handle your adversity is what people will look for and remember. I have heard it said multiple times that it only takes a moment to damage your reputation, but it takes years to build it back up. Avoid having to spend years rebuilding your relationships and reputation by taking ownership in doing the right thing all of the time.

It helps when you have positive reinforcement when taking risks and working in your talents. You should surround yourself with positive people and people who are going to encourage you. If members of your family are your biggest critics, limit your exposure to them. If your current friends are negative, make them your ex-friends and get some new ones. This may sound selfish or mean, but what are you doing for yourself by allowing negative energies to keep you from moving toward your dreams and effectively using your talents? You owe it to yourself to move forward, and if something or someone is holding you back, you need release those energies out of your surroundings. The people you spend time with should be of benefit to you, just as you should be a benefit to them.

> *"Don't get in your own way and don't let anyone else get in your way."*

Remember that God put the dream in your heart. Therefore, you are responsible to fulfill it. Don't get in your own way, and don't let anyone else get in your way. You do not need anyone else's permission to pursue what God put in you, so use these techniques or others that you may have discovered to defend against negative energies.

Before You Go...

Moving forward in living out your dreams and using your talents won't always be easy, so plan ahead with a strategy that you will use to defend against negativity. Keep positive people around you, remember inspiring quotes or scriptures, pray, and meditate.

Exposing Your Talents

Opportunities don't just happen—you have to make them happen with preparation, followed by action.

Exposing Your Talents

Don't sit down and wait for opportunities to come; you have to get up and make them.

—Madame CJ Walker

What is the good in having a talent if no one knows what you can do? Being shy about what you have to offer won't get you very far or give anyone confidence of your abilities to communicate effectively. Having others to communicate on your behalf is a good thing, but you should also be able to effectively showcase your capabilities. You have to give people a reason to promote you or be a reference for you. You need to let them know what you have to offer.

It can be easy to make the assumption that those who seem to get opportunity after opportunity have it easy and that things are just being handed to them. However, rewind their story. Odds are that they have produced in the past, they have delivered results and put forth the work to give people reason to provide them a chance. It starts with visibility and showing what you can do.

Visibility

If no one sees or knows what you are doing, it's hard to move forward with your goals and initiatives. And getting opportunities is nearly impossible in the workplace when no one knows what you are capable of doing.

Let others know what you can do: Nothing is wrong with tooting your own horn, if you have good reason to toot it. What are you good at? Good that you know. Now, does anyone else know that you are good at doing it? Let others know through word and deed what you are capable of doing. Everyone is busy, so most managers don't have time to investigate what you are up to. You should let your manager know not only what you have accomplished but also what you are interested in getting involved in.

Refine your skills: Just as you have to sharpen a knife to keep it properly functioning, you have to work toward keeping your talents sharpened. As mentioned in the "Investing in Your Talents" section of this book, you will find that there will be times when you need to do something to remain relevant and to keep your talent up-to-date. Why is this important when exposing your talents? Imagine yourself as a recruiter. At the beginning of your career, you were able to snag the best talent from simple recruiting techniques such as posting catchy help-wanted advertisements in the local newspapers, attending career fairs, and making cold calls. Today, if you are not equipped with the ability to use online social networks and the latest mobile technology, you are probably getting outpaced by the competition and not getting the best talent for your organization.

In order to stay up-to-date and competitive, you have to refine your talent. Find out what works, and then make it your own.

Volunteer with a nonprofit organization: Many nonprofit organizations are always in need of additional free assistance. This is a great way for you to serve others as well as enhance and expose your talents. Look for opportunities in your community and at your church or school. By doing this you are also able to determine if you truly have the talent or skill to be successful as well as to determine whether you need further development.

Volunteer for a project at work: In order to volunteer for projects at work, you have to be in the know about what's going on in the workplace. This may mean reading the company's newsletter or volunteering on teams. Of course you should stay in constant communication with your manager, who usually has a heads-up on pending projects. Plus, you need your manager's support to pursue the extra work. Before getting the opportunity, you will need to be a good performer in your role. So don't get lost doing the extra work over doing the necessary work.

Become a self-promoter: Don't be afraid to blow your own horn. However, show some restraint in order to not repel others from you. When you are trying to get a new opportunity, whether in your career or in some other area in your life, find out who the decision makers are so that you can express your interests and abilities with them. If they don't know who you are, it is hard to get in with them. When the opportunity presents itself, strike up meaningful conversations with those who can connect you with the right person.

Because aimless conversation can waste time—and, in some instances, resources, depending on how you are promoting yourself—be intentional when communicating with others. This is not saying that you should only communicate with those who can potentially provide you with opportunities, because you never know who can or will speak up for you. This just means that if you are pitching an idea, you want to make sure that it gets to the right person, whether that's from you directly or from someone who is willing to verbally sponsor you.

Remember that when you are in the presence of decision makers or their insiders, you should make sure that you strike up meaningful conversations. Always have a prepared message that you can express at a moment's notice. Some call it an elevator speech. Do you have one? If not, create a one-minute pitch.

Network: I caution you to not limit whom you network with. You have the opportunity to network with everyone you meet. You never know who holds a piece of information that can help you get over a difficult hurdle or the key to open up new opportunities for you.

Also, don't wait to network until you need something. You are too late if you take this approach. Be open-minded regarding whom you interact with, and be willing to collaborate with people who seem like an unlikely resource.

In the workplace, people say, the same people are always being asked to participate on exciting projects or teams. Why is that? Probably because some in management don't want to take a risk on the lesser-known employee. The same holds true in other organizations as well, from church to school and social organizations. There is a lot of untapped knowledge that is never discovered because the people who hold the knowledge

"Find the proper balance to let others know who you are and what you can do."

are overlooked because of the "what do they know" or "whom do they know" questions. So, what do you know, and whom do you know? And yes, it is true that who you know can get you in places that you can't get to on your own.

Before You Go...

Be willing to be vulnerable and show others that you have the capabilities to be successful. People want to know your track record before they trust you with valuable resources of time and money. Find the proper balance to let others know who you are and what you can do.

Embrace Who You Are

Get out of your head and get to work!

Embrace Who You Are

Have confidence that if you have done a little thing well,
you can do a bigger thing well, too.

—Joseph Storey

You are a unique being! You can search far and wide and may find someone with similar characteristics, but you will never find an exact match.

When you embrace your unique self, you are accepting who you are, with your perceived imperfections and all. It takes some an entire lifetime to accept who they are. Don't wait that long. God didn't make a mistake on any of us, and once you believe that, it is easier to embrace who you are and what you have to offer.

Don't mistake your imperfections for the bad habits that you may possess. If you are someone who neglects to pick up after yourself, that's not an imperfection; that's a bad habit. Or if you are someone who resorts to whining in order to get someone to do something for you, that is not the power of persuasion or negotiation; that is selfishness—and, to be blunt, childish. Hiding the truth to close a deal doesn't describe a good or natural salesperson; what that describes is a deceitful one. Do you get the picture? These are bad habits that get picked up over time and can become hard to break if they aren't corrected—and they are not talents by any means. That's not what I am referring to here.

Take Time to Understand What You Have to Offer

So what are some characteristics you may have that are actually hidden talents or skills that you should embrace? It's likely that someone else pointed these out to you, but maybe not in a positive context. Here are some examples of characteristics that may annoy others that you may try to overshadow because of what others may think:

- Are you someone who notices something wrong in a situation that others think is just fine, and you are not satisfied until you discover more? If so, you may find yourself as being an investigator or researcher.
- Are you someone who debates about any subject matter? If so, you may find yourself as being a politician, lawyer or advocate.

- Are you someone who can talk to anyone about anything? If so, you may find yourself as being a public speaker, counselor, or minister.

- Are you someone who can find humor in almost any situation? If so, you may find yourself as being a comedian or comedic writer.

- Are you someone who speaks up, even when you are not asked? If so, you may find yourself as being a social worker, child advocate or social activist.

- Are you someone who constantly looks for a better way to accomplish a task, even when a solution is found? If so, you may find yourself as being an inventor, innovator, researcher, engineer, or entrepreneur.

- Are you someone who daydreams or are a great "storyteller" to fill in the gaps of the unknown? If so, you may find yourself as being an author, film writer, or playwright.

- Are you someone who will draw on any flat surface near you if you are sitting around long enough? If so, you may find yourself as being an artist, animator, or graphic designer.

- Are you someone who looks for opportunities to share your advice with anyone who will listen? If so, you may find yourself as being a psychologist, psychiatrist, or counselor.

- Are you someone who takes something that is working properly apart, just to see how it works, and puts it back together again? If so, you may find yourself as being an engineer, electrician, or mechanic.

These are just some examples, and the list can go on and on. The point is that some of the things that you do that may annoy others could be your gateway to finding out where your natural talents reside. When you embrace these characteristics, you may find opportunities to develop them into worthwhile talents that can benefit you and others.

Consider Feedback from Others

Sometimes others have to point out what we are good at that is not so obvious to us. Have you ever had someone ask you if you have ever tried, or would you like to try some specific activity? For example, I went to see one of my former instructors after I found out that she was retiring. We caught up with our recent activities, and then she asked me if I had ever thought about teaching. I have wanted to teach since I was in elementary school, but more recently, I was thinking about what it would take to teach at the college level. I told her this, and she immediately introduced me to her boss, and we got the ball rolling. It all happened quickly and was unexpected to me.

What would have given her the notion to ask me such a question? My best guess is that in her classes, I had several presentation assignments where I scored really high grades, and maybe to her, that translated to me being capable to instruct students. Or it could have been something else totally. I didn't ask her why she asked, I was just honored that she did. I now have several semesters of teaching experience and have realized that the childhood desire is still there. Throughout my teaching experience, I have received good ratings and was asked to come back on multiple occasions. Additionally, former students have thanked me for what they got out of my class.

Even in my full-time position, I find myself looking for the opportunity to facilitate or coach, even in small doses, because every experience counts. If you keep hearing you're good at "something," I encourage you to take a closer look at it. Everyone may not agree that you are good, but you owe it to yourself to explore it.

In embracing who you are, you must be willing to accept coaching from those who have your best interest in mind. Sometimes the coaching that we receive is a hard reality to swallow, but in order to make the most of who you are, you need to have an understanding of certain characteristics. Coaching isn't meant to change you but rather to smooth out the rough edges and refine who you are.

You can view coaching similar to the process a diamond goes through.

Diamonds are the hardest substance found, and they need to be shaped so that when they are presented, they are at their best. A diamond is mostly known for its beauty as a gemstone. However, diamonds have many uses in other industries. You should consider yourself the same. You are more than what is on the outside. There is more within you that needs to be explored and shaped. Discover how you can make the most out of what you have and who you are.

You are valuable, and so are your talents, if you choose to take the time to figure out how to use them. Look at it this way. In your uncoached state, consider your talents a diamond in the rough. Your talents carry high value that is waiting to be discovered. It will take time for exploration to discover them, and sometimes what was thought to be a talent may be something else. Don't give up; it's a process. Once your talent is discovered, there is more for you to do, which you may find painful. You may have to go through trial and error to figure out what you've got. Some of the things you try may not work, but you will find that it

> *"You are valuable, and so are your talents, if you choose to take the time to figure out how to use them."*

is worth the effort. Dig up your talent, shape and refine your talent, and then show off its beauty to the world.

There is Value in What You Have to Offer

Your perceived imperfections do not lessen the value of who you are. If you take damaged paper currency and deposit it in the bank, the value is still the same as long as it is recognizable and authentic. So figure out what you have, embrace it and make it work for you.

Before You Go...

Don't hide behind insecurities. Your payoff will come in loving yourself and being confident in what you have to offer. If you properly prepare yourself and learn from previous experiences you are giving yourself a better chance at being successful.

Stay Out of Trouble

Sometimes letting go is hard, but holding on can be detrimental.

Stay Out of Trouble

If I take care of my character, my reputation will take care of itself.

—*Dwight L. Moody*

Life is hard enough as it is, so why create trouble for yourself? Surprisingly, there are many people who have found that the trouble they got into when they were younger somehow finds a way back into their present. You are not afraid to use your talents, but others are afraid to be around you because of your behavior or your attitude.

When you were in school, getting into trouble may have made your classmates laugh or turned you into the popular kid in school. Your teachers may have shaken their heads and thought to themselves that you were at it again and sent you to the principal's office. Despite all of that, you were still allowed to continue your education and eventually graduate. When you become an adult, your troubles are not as easy to overcome as when you were in school. Depending on the type of trouble that you may find yourself in, it could lead to you not fulfilling your destiny or doing what you truly desire.

It's unfortunate to see so many talented individuals finding themselves on the outside looking in, scraping the bottom of the barrel because of a handful of bad decisions. Unfortunately, acts of immaturity can steer you off in the wrong direction.

Trouble doesn't just occur in your youth or to those in certain types of jobs or to those in low socioeconomic statuses. Don't think you are too old, too rich, or positioned too high in your organization to get into trouble. Trouble can happen at any age and wherever you go. No one is immune, so be alert.

So what does trouble have to do with your talents? Easy. If you are constantly in trouble or get yourself in big trouble, how are you going to use your talents effectively? Also, who will want to work with you? Getting into trouble isn't just reserved for going to jail, getting kicked out of school, or getting terminated. So what could trouble look like?

Trouble Spots

Having a bad attitude: Take heed to the warnings about your attitude. I have heard before that good people skills can get you far in your career. Or maybe you have heard that you can attract more bees with honey. Either way you heard it, the message is that your attitude is in direct correlation to your success. People are more willing to help you develop or grow in your career if you exhibit the right attitude.

It's not easy to define a good attitude, because it is largely based on perception and culture. It takes longer to determine whether someone has a bad attitude. So what is a bad attitude? Unfortunately, it's hard to define, because what some consider a bad attitude, others see as being assertive or being a good leader. However, some common attributes are as follows:

- Talking over others
- Not taking direction, not listening
- Being argumentative
- Being negative or the office gossip
- Disruptive actions or sabotaging others
- Being disrespectful or overly outspoken
- Refusing to work or participate in team efforts
- Starting fights, not being able to keep the peace
- Using profanity, being rude

- Doing your own thing with no regard for others

Making questionable decisions: If you are of the mind-set that you need to get ahead by any means necessary, that can quickly get you into trouble. Don't resort to doing things that you know are against the rules in order to get ahead. Some say that "rules are meant to be broken." However, some broken rules can cost you money or your freedom. Before you fall into the temptation of making questionable decisions, ask yourself: Will this damage my reputation? What will it really cost? What punishment can come with this? Is the risk worth the reward? It's probably not.

Don't put yourself on the path of growing a bad reputation. Consistent bad behavior on your part will lead to people not wanting to have anything to do with you. You see this in sports. Many talented athletes get into trouble on or off the field and then find themselves out of the league because of their behavior. Recently, a football player who left college with such promise was released from the professional team that drafted him. His off-the-field behavior didn't represent the image that the league or team wanted to tolerate. In his situation, all press wasn't good press; and in his case, it likely has caused him to lose out of millions of dollars.

There is a cable television program that focuses on individuals who used their positions or intelligence to cheat the system or to scam others. It amazes me when I watch because many of these individuals were really smart and talented and would have likely attained major success if they had chosen a legal or honest means for earning an income. However, their choices—or rather, questionable decisions—landed them in prison. No one wins in the end when others set out in deceptive activities.

Stirring up confusion in your environment: No one really likes a gossip, and most don't trust them, either. If you don't rest when there is peace, or you are bringing negative attention to others, you are wasting significant time when you can be productive. There are *at least three* issues in stirring up confusion.

1. You are making something out of nothing and creating unnecessary conflicts.
2. You are ruining someone else's reputation.
3. You are causing others to not want to work with you.

When you are having conversations about others, are you helping to resolve the issue, or are you making it worse? Does the situation you are speaking about have anything to do with you? If not, why are you discussing it? You should spend time discussing your qualities and attributes and expressing ways you can help resolve problems.

When you find yourself involved in gossip, figure out a way to turn the subject around to your talents, interests, and what you have to offer. Stop spreading rumors. Stop being the bearer of bad news. Think about it. While you are throwing someone in the mud, you can't help but get some on you.

Lying, cheating, or stealing: Bad, bad, bad! These are three attributes that can flush your reputation down the toilet immediately. All of these things create major damage to your integrity. We all probably know a good storyteller, someone who can make the most boring event colorful enough to make you wish you were there. We also may know someone who bends the truth in order to cover something up or to make him- or herself look like the hero. Don't try to be the hero if you truly weren't. Don't take credit for what you didn't do or hide your mistakes. Taking credit for someone else's work is stealing. The truth somehow always comes out in the end, and your reputation takes a hit when others find out. Put forth the effort to figure things out for yourself. Don't cheat your way through school or through life. Taking shortcuts and producing low-quality work is cheating. Cheating stunts your growth and prevents you from developing and fully utilizing your talents.

Constantly making excuses: Who is the person involved in all of your endeavors? Easy, it's you. When you succeed, you are there. When you fail, you are there. When you make mistakes or miss deadlines, you are there. It's OK to make mistakes as long as you learn from them. Mistakes will happen, but when they happen, don't make excuses. Own up to them and figure out how to avoid making the same mistakes again in the future.

Though it may be true that others may get in the way of you achieving your goals, you must find a way to overcome. Blaming someone else or finger pointing is no good excuse for not continuously striving to do better.

As we know, excuses come in many forms, because most of us have either heard or made them. Some make the excuse that they don't have the support from their families, teachers, managers, or whomever, which is why they haven't achieved more in their lives. You should take ownership of your life and your goals. Having support is important, but not having it should not keep you from moving forward in accomplishing goals. Find the inner strength within yourself to move forward, and eventually support will come.

People attribute where they are from as a reason for the lack of opportunity. Although there are barriers that may be presented as a result of the location of your neighborhood, you should look for opportunities to eliminate the barriers. I grew up in a rural neighborhood where resources were limited. However, self-determination and advancements in technology can help you figure out how to overcome most barriers. Use what is available to you. Don't give up just because you face challenges without first looking for ways to get help.

Even parents sometimes say things like, "If I didn't have children, then I could," or "I have to focus my time on my children, so I don't have time to focus on my goals." STOP! Becoming a parent can send you on a detour or halt your progress, but I challenge you to find a way to fit in using your talents. Even small accomplishments will help you get there. By keeping your eye on the prize, you are not just working on bettering your future, but you are serving as an example to your children by showing will and determination. Making excuses won't earn you any rewards or lead you to success. Get over it and move on.

Choosing not to listen to sound advice: Have you ever felt like someone sounds like a broken record? It seems like you keep hearing the same thing over and over again. Sometimes you want to scream "Shut up!" to whomever that person is because you are so tired of hearing what he or she has to say. Guess what. That person will at some point get tired of having to tell you the same thing over and over again.

If you keep hearing the same type of unfavorable feedback from multiple sources, you may want to take a step back and assess the critiques. There's a possibility that you may need to change or adjust your behavior. If someone who has your best interest in mind continuously gives you advice on areas of improvement, and you ignore that person's recommendations, it is likely that he or she will eventually give up on trying to help you. One thing you don't want is for people to lose interest in helping you to develop personally or professionally.

Being judgmental toward others: If you have enough time to peek into someone else's situation to be judgmental toward him or her, then you are probably not spending enough time working on your own situation. The more time you spend picking someone else apart, the less time you have to better yourself. Plus, being judgmental toward *"Do you want to be known for your troubles or for your talents?"* others is a sign of your own insecurity. You are not making yourself better by being negative toward others. The next time you find yourself being judgmental, ask yourself what you are hoping to accomplish by doing so.

In the end, you don't want to let your trouble define you, and you don't want it to linger. The question you can ask yourself is: Do you want to be known for your troubles or for your talents? Getting into trouble or exhibiting bad behavior can lead to shaping an image of yourself that is unflattering and may cause you to get overlooked for exciting opportunities. Don't let your troubles cast a gloomy shadow over your talents.

I am willing to bet that most people have gotten into a little bit of trouble at some point in their lives, because no one is perfect. Having someone in your life to hold you accountable can help you figure out how to avoid or minimize the impact of any trouble that you might find yourself in.

There is a direct relationship between your behaviors and your reputation. If you are not sure of your reputation, ask someone whom you trust for feedback, whether it's your pastor, parents, teacher, manager, or mentor. We all have blind spots, and they are blind spots because they are not easily recognized by inner reflection. Because of this, it will take others shedding light on these behaviors for you.

Before You Go...

The short-term gains of trouble won't last long before you find yourself in another similar situation. Eventually, if you find yourself continuously getting into trouble, getting out can be costly, including you missing out on life changing opportunities. Before you find yourself doing something that doesn't seem right to you, be sure to ask yourself what it will cost you once all is said and done.

Finding Your Inspiration

Look deep within yourself to find the
purpose in everything you do.

Finding Your Inspiration

Real success is finding your lifework in the work that you love.

—*David McCullough*

As you journey through life, you are going to face obstacles, interact with people who don't believe in your dreams, or have to combat against negative energies. Despite all of that, you must keep your eyes on what's ahead. You may get some quick wins, but don't lose sight of your overall goal.

Before heading in and committing yourself to your mission, make sure you know what's behind your desires. You don't want a bunch of false starts, because that can become discouraging. What will inspire you to keep moving forward when times get tough? You may find that it is going to take more than pure talent to keep you going. We live in a very competitive world, and because of this, you are likely to face adversity—in some instances from people, or in situations, that you may not have expected.

So ask yourself: Why am I doing this? Why is this important to me? If you are doing something "just because," you will stop doing it and move on to something else "just because" when things get tough.

When you wake up in the morning and start your day, are you getting dressed for work just because? You may not like your job, but you are going to it for a reason. There has to be a reason. Otherwise, if you have no reason to do anything, then why bother to get out of the bed in the first place? So, other than the obvious, why do you get out of bed? Have you asked yourself that question lately?

People are inspired to achieve a certain goal for a number of reasons. However, stay away from wanting to reach a certain status to prove something (your capabilities) to someone else. Though you can use that as a catalyst, you should desire success because you want it for yourself. What happens when the fans go away, and your status fades? If you are setting goals for yourself, this isn't a factor.

As mentioned, everyone is not going to believe in you. If you live your life trying to prove something, then where are you going to get your happiness? There will always be someone else to prove something as well. People who doubt you will see your worth when you achieve the success that you really want, so there is no need to prove anything to anyone. Let your self-driven achievements speak for themselves.

So again, what's your inspiration? What's driving you? What's pushing you when you feel you have nothing left?

Your Spiritual Connection with God

God has plans for us, and He will show mercy on us and provide direction for us if we seek Him. "For I know the thoughts that I think toward you, says the LORD, thoughts of peace and not of evil, to give you a future and a hope. And you will seek Me and find Me, when you search for Me with all your heart" (Jeremiah 29:11, 13).

When you find that you are struggling and feel there is nothing left to turn to, go to the Bible and find one of the many promises there to lift your spirits and remind you that you have a future and a hope. Pray and ask God for direction, and you will find that a new idea, thought, direction, or opportunity may present itself to you that will help get you out of your rut.

Having a Deep Personal Desire

It is important to measure success based on your own beliefs and desires. It will mean more to you to accomplish something because it is a desire of your heart versus living up to someone else's goals for you. Plus, if you are doing something you love, whether you are paid for it or not, it will not feel like work. You may find that what you have a deep personal desire to do will not lead to a paycheck, but it will lead to the internal reward of personal fulfillment.

Special Interest

Sometimes you find that the talent you are possessed with can help further the efforts of an organization or some special interest that you have. When you have the passion to make a difference, you are likely to want to see those efforts pay off. Therefore, the urge to push yourself and "put your best foot forward," so to speak, will compel you to dig in and let your talents shine.

Overcoming Fear or a Setback

One thing that paralyzes many, as it relates to living out their potential, is fear, whether it's fear of trying because you are afraid to fail or fear of trying again because you failed before. Fear has kept many on the sidelines, so if you find yourself there, you are not alone. Use that fear to energize yourself to move forward. Even if you don't hit the objective that you set out to accomplish, if you put forth your best effort, you are sure to gain some type of learning through the experience.

If going after your goals won't kill you, why should you let fear rule your life? From my experience, I have organized and sponsored two events that were visible for many to see if they failed. The events were successful in that they were well organized and served the purpose that I set out for them to accomplish, but the attendance

"Your past can be your best inspiration to keep you moving forward!"

was low. Because of this, the events could be seen as failures, and for a while this result caused me to hesitate to move forward on other initiatives because I was focusing on the financial loss. As I didn't die from the experience, I was able to reflect on what I learned in order to apply those learnings to other projects. Instead of thinking about what you can lose, become motivated by what you can gain. Financially, I lost a lot of money with those events, but I gained valuable experience.

Each milestone that you achieve will help boost your confidence to go further. This will help because if you face a difficult challenge on the journey, you will have the opportunity to look at how far you've come. Eventually, the road that got you to where you are will be a collection of confidence boosters when you look back to see what you have overcome. Your past can be your best inspiration to keep you moving forward!

Unhappiness in Your Current Situation

When you are unhappy in your current situation, you should change your situation. However, before changing your situation, you should first understand what is causing you to be unhappy. Knowing what is causing your unhappiness will help you avoid the potential time bomb of unhappiness in a new situation. When you read about entrepreneurs, some level of unhappiness is what caused them to change their situations in starting their own businesses. Maybe starting your own business isn't for you, but what will changing your situation do for you?

Financial Gain or Social Status

Money, power, and respect are motivators for many, and some hope to accomplish these things by any means necessary. Money, power, and respect can get you a lot of things, but does it lead you to personal fulfillment and genuine happiness? You may be using your God-given talents, but don't get so fixated on the financial gain and social status that comes with it that you depend on it to keep you happy.

There are many examples of those who enjoyed the luxuries of being rich and famous who ended up losing it all when the next big thing came out and they weren't prepared for it. There is a balancing act that must occur in order to continuously enjoy the fruits of your labor and be true to yourself. Only you can determine the correct balance for yourself.

Before You Go...

Having the desire to do something is great, but the purpose behind the desire is what will keep you going. Keep the inspiration in mind so that when things get a little tough, or a lot tough, you won't quit, because what inspires you will serve as a motivation to get you through.

What's Next?

Put one foot in front of the other, and go for it, whatever it is.

What's Next?

It is our attitude at the beginning of a difficult task which more than anything else will affect its successful outcome.

—William James

Shortly after I completed my undergraduate degree, I contemplated pursuing my graduate degree. I told this to one of my coworkers and was asked what I was waiting for. I didn't have a good answer, but the response I received was that the time would pass whether I went back to school or not. And yes, the time did continue to go on. I didn't go back to school for my graduate degree for an additional eight years. Going back was exciting for me, although challenging, but two years later, I celebrated earning my graduate degree.

I finally went for it and can add that to my list of accomplishments as I continue to work on sharpening my skills to use my talents. My push to finish this book was inspired by my push to finish the multiple papers and projects that were required for my most recent degree program. I used that same energy and drive as a reminder that even though it may seem daunting, I can do it. Use whatever is necessary to motivate yourself to move forward.

Believe in Yourself

I spoke with one of my former coworkers who told me about his desire to write music. He informed me about how he would throw away what he created before finishing because he didn't think it was good enough. His situation reminded me of my drawing situation, with the difference being that he was the one criticizing his work versus the criticism coming from someone else.

He had a lot of negative self-talk going on in his mind, even when speaking with me about it. I did my best to encourage him during that short conversation and recommended that he create a "to review" folder so that he could store his work there instead of throwing it away.

Success begins in the mind. You have to be able to encourage yourself and be your biggest cheerleader. Even if at first you are not successful at something or pleased with your output, mimic a professional athlete and have a short-term memory about the mistake and get back in the game.

You are already equipped to get started using your talents. So if you have hidden them, get out your mental shovel and dig them out, dust them off, and develop a plan on how you are going to use them.

So what is it in life that you need to go for? What talents do you have that you will no longer be afraid to use? By using your talents, I believe you have more to gain than to lose. There are plenty of examples throughout history and in our present times of those who have pushed past doubters, discouragement, and challenges to live out their dreams and desires.

You are on a continuous journey in life. Each stage in your life is connected to the previous stage. Consider each phase or experience in your life as a link on a chain. Each link belongs to you and is on a continuum. You will share these experiences with others, but each experience belongs to you, and those experiences will not have the same impact on others as they have on you. Others can influence certain phases in your life, but they can't live your life, just as you can't live the life of someone else. I encourage you to not allow the influences of others to keep you from living out your dreams and going for the desires of your heart.

Go For It

About fifteen years ago, I came across a wood carving that states, "Go for it! Life is not a dress rehearsal." I loved the statement and had to purchase the art. Apparently many people like this quote as well, because I have seen it quoted so many times that I don't know whom to give proper credit to for pinning it. However, Rose Tremain seems like the likely source. Either way, you are encouraged to go for it. Or you can do as my high-school motto states, and that is to carpe diem—seize the day! Because you don't know what tomorrow may bring, you owe it to yourself to go for it and to seize the day. I wish you the best on your journey as you live your life unafraid of using your talents!

Some Quick Tips…

- Define success on your own terms.
- Don't stop growing and developing your talent.
- Look for ways to improve your talents.
- Explore multiple ways to use your talents.
- Be willing to adjust how you use your talents.
- Stay connected with those you can learn from.
- Remember that your talents need updating, just as technology needs updating.
- In order to stay current/relevant, you must continue to learn.

- Get rid of the background noise that's creating distractions.
- Prepare for what's ahead!

Before You Go...

- Your talents are gifts.
- Your talents are blessings.
- Your talents are uniquely yours.
- Your talents belong to you.
- Your talents are waiting to be unleashed.

Application

When you reach your initial goal of success, you must continue to work at staying successful.

What is your definition of success?

What does it (success) look like? (What are you doing or what did you do to get there?)

Whom can you contact to begin a mentoring relationship?

What do you want to gain from having a mentor?

What types of activities will you use to stay positive?

What is your greatest accomplishment from the past twelve months?

Write down opportunities for you to expose your talents.

When the opportunity presents itself, write down your key selling points.

What is it about you that stands out more than anything else about you?

How can this characteristic be used to enhance your talents?

How will you smooth out your rough edges?

What behaviors do you exhibit that could hinder you from moving forward in developing your talent?

Write down situations that trigger your bad behavior and how you will adjust reactions.

Write down how you get inspired to move forward.

What talent have you hidden that you will now start using?

Talents All Around

Presenting   Problem Solving   Designing
Driving Researching   Collaborating
Athletic Carpentry Facilitating Improvising
Making People Laugh   Entertaining
Repairing Innovating   Caring for Others
Coordinating   Persuading

Troubleshooting
Analyzing Acting
Leading Directing
Editing Communicating
Negotiating Drawing
Teaching Preaching
Speaking Advising

TALENTS

Creative Builder
Organizing Orator
Supporting
Explaining
Hair Stylist
Cooking Producing
Hunter Dancing
Writing
Artistic
Farmer
Musician
Coaching

What's your talent?

About the Author

Shawnté Jones is a member of the Grace United Methodist Church in Brazoria, TX, where she is an active member in addition to writing and publishing a quarterly newsletter. She holds a bachelor's of arts degree in communication from the University of Houston-Clear Lake and a master's of science degree in human resource development from the University of Houston.

Shawnté is the youngest of seven children by her parents, David and Gracie Jones, and she enjoys spending time with her family and friends.

Shawnté looks forward to the opportunity to provide inspiration and encouragement to others because she believes that all people have something within them that makes them great.

See more about what Shawnté is up to by visiting www.thebeboldenterprises.com.

37571454R00068

Made in the USA
San Bernardino, CA
20 August 2016